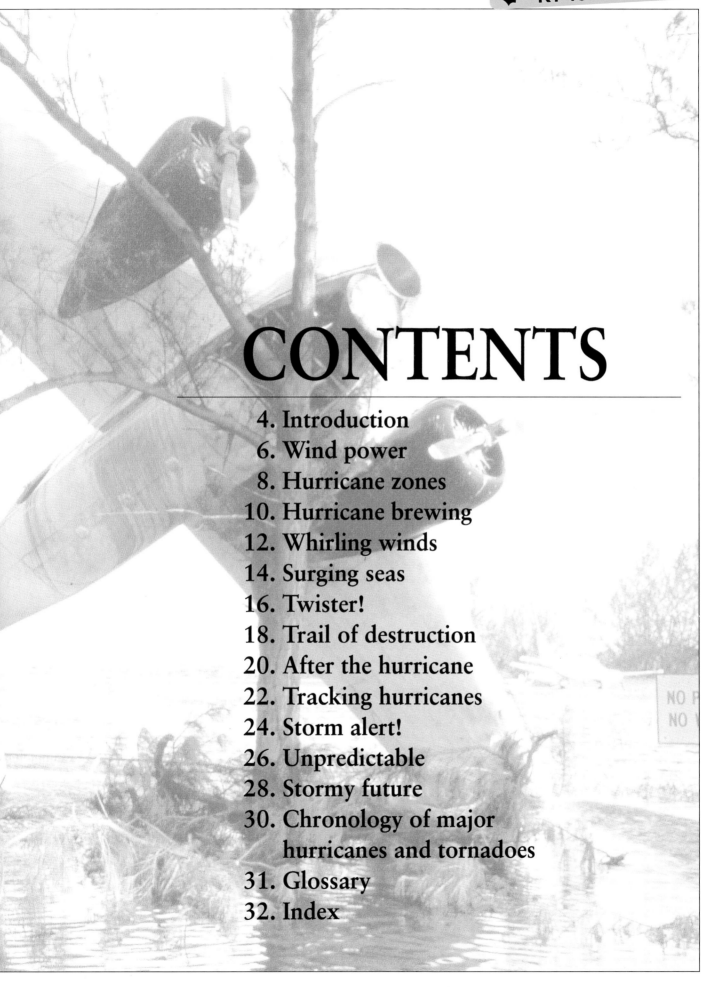

CONTENTS

INTRODUCTION

Hurricanes are violent, spinning storms with towering thunderclouds and torrential rains. Inside a hurricane, screaming winds rotate at high speed around a calm, cloudless area in the centre, called the "eye". Hurricanes are many times more powerful than ordinary thunderstorms. Forming over tropical oceans, they whip up giant waves. Most hurricanes rage harmlessly at sea. Some cause great damage if they reach land. Hurricanes cause massive devastation every year, flattening towns, uprooting forests and taking many lives.

NCOJ

CLOSER LOOK AT

ANES
HOONS

Jen Green

Franklin Watts
LONDON ● SYDNEY

An Aladdin Book
© Aladdin Books Ltd 1996
Designed and produced by
Aladdin Books Ltd
28 Percy Street
London W1P 0LD

First published in Great Britain
in 1996 by
Franklin Watts
96 Leonard Street
London EC2A 4XD

ISBN: 0 7496 2475 2 (hb)
ISBN: 0 7496 3581 9 (pb)

Editor
Alex Edmonds

Designer
Gary Edgar-Hyde

Picture Research
Brooks Krikler Research

Illustrators
Ian Moores
Creative Hands and Aziz Khan
Guy Smith
Ian Thompson

Certain illustrations have appeared in
earlier books created by Aladdin Books.

Consultant
Jane Insley is curator of the meteorology collection at
the Science Museum, London, where she researches
and writes about the history and current practice of
weather and climate studies.

5

Bad weather blues

An area of low pressure, where air rises, is called a depression. As the air in a depression moves around, belts of cloud and rain, called fronts, move with it. Areas of warm air are rising over cold air to produce the movement. In a warm front, warm air meets cold air and rises slowly, producing light rain. In a cold front, cold air moves under warm air. This pushes up the warm air rapidly and heavy rains usually follow.

Measuring wind

Wind speed is measured by the Beaufort scale, named after Admiral Beaufort who invented it in 1805. The first scale described the effects of wind at sea, but it has since been given symbols and adapted for land. Force 12 is a wind over 117kph, called "hurricane-strength", but this does not mean the wind was caused by a hurricane.

Our planet is surrounded by a thick layer of air called the atmosphere. The air in the atmosphere is always moving. Winds are currents of warm and cold air, which move across the surface of the Earth and up and down in the atmosphere. Around the world, winds blow in regular patterns, caused by the action of the Sun heating the air.

WIND

Warm air

Warm front

Warm area

Cold front

Cold area

Cold air

BENDING THE WINDS

Our planet is spinning round from west to east. The spin is fastest at the Equator, more than 1000 km per hour. The paths of the world's winds are bent by the Earth's spin. Rather than blowing north-south from the Equator to the Poles, they curve almost parallel to the Equator. This is called the Coriolis effect. As the map shows, on either side of the Equator the winds blow from east to west. Towards the Poles they blow from west to east.

Trade winds that blow from the north-east

Hurricanes

Area of light winds called the Doldrums

1 Calm – Smoke rises vertically

2 Slight breeze – Smoke drifts

3 Gentle breeze – Leaves rustle

4 Moderate breeze – Twigs move

5 Fresh breeze – Waves form small crests

Plants have developed different ways of protecting themselves from powerful winds. Palm trees grow mainly in tropical parts of the world, where hurricanes sometimes occur. Their flexible trunks bend and spring back in high winds, but rarely break.

POWER

Wind cells

Because of the curved shape of the Earth, the Sun's rays are strongest at the Equator and weakest at the Poles. Air heated near the Equator rises and moves towards the Poles. Cooler air rushes in to replace it. As the warm air cools, it sinks back to Earth again. This creates a circular flow of air, called a wind cell. There are five great bands of wind cells circling the Earth, one at the Equator and each of the Poles, and two in the temperate regions in between.

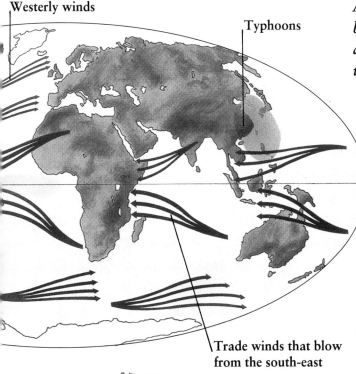

Westerly winds

Typhoons

Trade winds that blow from the south-east

Cold air moves towards the equator.

Air heated at the equator rises towards the poles.

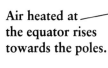

6 Strong breeze – Wind whistles in telephone wires

7 Near gale – Whole trees sway

8 Gale – It is difficult to walk

9 Strong gale – Tiles are blown from roofs

10 Storm – Trees are uprooted

11 Violent storm – Buildings are damaged

12 Hurricane – Devastation is caused

Hurricanes occur in the tropical regions near the Equator. They develop over warm oceans where seawater warmed by the Sun evaporates to form huge storm clouds. As the warm air rises, cooler air replaces it, creating a wind. The rotation of the Earth bends the wind inwards, causing it to rotate and spiral upwards with great force.

HURRICANE

In the heart of the hurricane
Inside a hurricane such as Hurricane Ellen in the Atlantic (above), winds turn clockwise in the Southern Hemisphere and anticlockwise in the Northern Hemisphere. These swirling masses of air spin faster and faster, until wind speed exceeds 120kph – hurricane strength. Driven by the wind, the hurricane begins to travel across the Earth's surface at a speed of up to 50kph.

HURRICANES AROUND THE WORLD

Hurricanes are known by different names in various parts of the world. In the Atlantic Ocean and the Caribbean they are called hurricanes. In the Pacific Ocean they are generally known as Typhoons, and on the right we see typhoon Unsang, in the Philippines. In the Indian Ocean they are called tropical cyclones. Hurricanes may measure as much as 300 kilometres across. Some are even larger. Such a storm takes a long time to pass.

ON CLOSER INSPECTION
– *Hurricane names*

The man who first gave names to hurricanes was C.Wragge, an Australian weather forecaster of the early 1900s. Elsewhere, hurricanes and tornados such as this unnamed one that struck in Florida, USA in 1926, did not get names until later this century.

ZONES

AN A TO Z OF HURRICANES

Nowadays hurricanes are also given individual names to make them easier to track and identify. The names work alphabetically; the first hurricane of the year is given a name beginning with the letter "A", the second with "B", and so on. At one time all the names used were female, but they are now male and female alternately!

Hurricanes form in warm waters near the Equator. The arrows below show the paths of these storms. Hurricanes do not occur in the South Atlantic Ocean, where the waters are too cold for them to form.

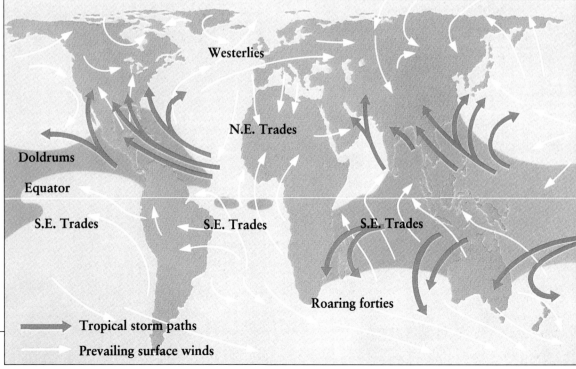

Westerlies

N.E. Trades

Doldrums

Equator

S.E. Trades   S.E. Trades   S.E. Trades

Roaring forties

→ Tropical storm paths
→ Prevailing surface winds

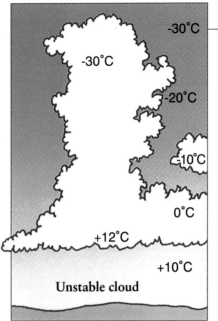

-30°C
-30°C
-20°C
-10°C
0°C
+12°C
+10°C

Unstable cloud

-10°C
-5°C
0°C
-2°C
+5°C
+12°C
+10°C

Stable cloud

rom June to November it is hurricane season in the Atlantic Ocean and tropical cyclone time in the Indian Ocean. The seas are at their warmest in these hot, humid (moist) conditions. Thunderclouds appear, from which tropical storms can develop. Sun, sky and sea are ready to combine in Earth's most violent chain reaction.

HURRICANE

BIRTH OF A HURRICANE

In the Atlantic Ocean hurricanes are often started by an easterly wave (blue arrows), an area of low pressure. At first this is weak, producing rain showers (1). But sometimes ocean winds, called trade winds (red arrows), and high-altitude winds may combine to strengthen the wave, creating seedling storms (2) which may build into a tropical storm (3).

Clouds

As warm air rises, it cools and the moisture in it condenses to form clouds. If air around the cloud is warmer than the cloud, stable, or unchanging, clouds form, (see bottom diagram). If the rising air is warmer than the air around it, it rises to a great height, forming an unstable cloud called a cumulonimbus (see top diagram). These heavy, black clouds may warn of a thunderstorm.

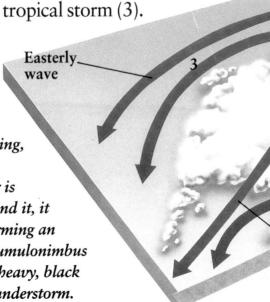

Easterly wave

3

Trade winds

Tropical storm

On Closer Inspection
– *Hurricanes in space*

Hurricanes exist elsewhere in our Solar System too. The Red Spot on Jupiter, the largest planet in the Solar System, is larger than the Earth in size. This spot is actually the top of a spiral storm or cyclone in Jupiter's gas, which has raged for more than 300 years.

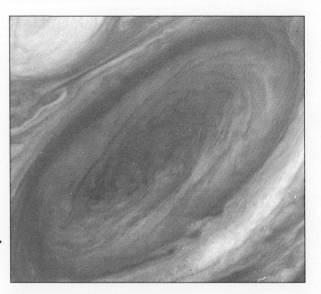

BREWING

Easterly wave

Thunderstorm

1

2

Zone around
the equator

Seedling
storm

Easterly wave winds are named after the direction from which they blow. So a wind blowing from the east is called an easterly.

How stormclouds form

All air contains some water vapour – water in the form of gas. In tropical regions, the Sun heats the oceans, evaporating seawater, to become water vapour in the air. The warm air above tropical seas becomes charged with water vapour. As the warm air rises, it cools and the water vapour turns into tiny drops of water, which form clouds. The progress of these storm clouds can be viewed by satellites which can take pictures such as the one below, of the eye, or centre of the storm.

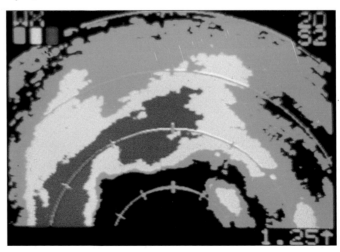

The calm eye

At the centre of the hurricane is the "eye", an area up to 30km wide. The eye is cloudless, with only a light breeze. The few people who have survived being caught in the storm's eye say that if they looked up, they could see the stars, and walls of rotating cloud around them.

Once warm air in a tropical storm spirals upwards, a chain reaction could turn the storm into a hurricane. Water vapour in the rising air condenses, releasing heat. As the air warms, it spirals up even faster, reaching high speeds around the centre. More air is drawn in at the bottom and blown out at the top.

WHIRLING

THE HURRICANE RAGES

Pictures cannot show the full fury of a hurricane. Wind speeds may exceed 200 kph around the central eye, powerful enough to drive a piece of straw through a wooden plank. Occasional gusts may reach 300 kph. Towns can be ripped from the land and small countries entirely devastated by these raging winds. Torrential rain pours down and winds lash the sea, creating terrifying giant waves.

The photo on the left shows Hurricane Gilbert reaching the Gulf of Mexico. This was one of the most powerful hurricanes ever recorded, with winds gusting to 320kph. Hurricane Gilbert struck the West Indies and Mexico in 1988.

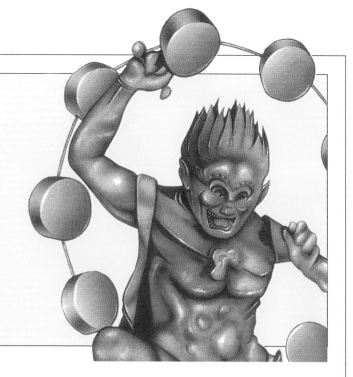

WINDS

Inside the calm, central eye, cool air descends (red arrow).

Air spirals upwards around the centre of the storm (pink arrows) and swirls outwards at the top (blue arrows).

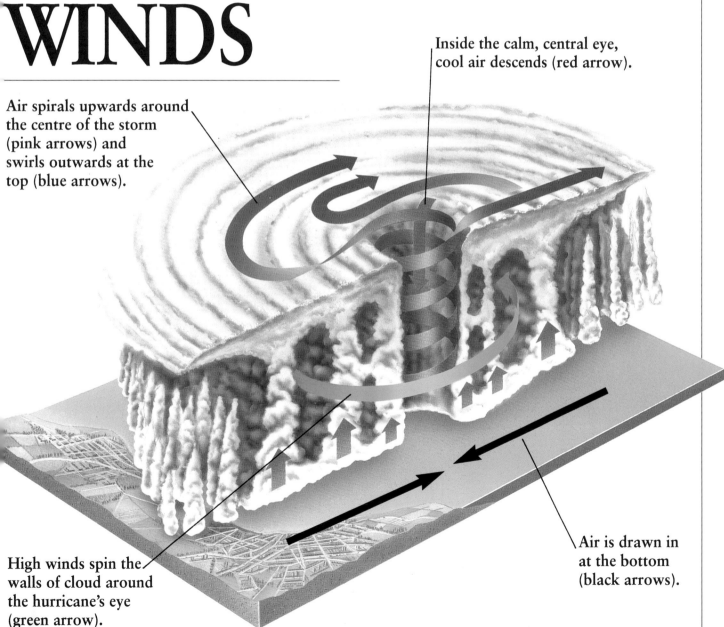

High winds spin the walls of cloud around the hurricane's eye (green arrow).

Air is drawn in at the bottom (black arrows).

13

Philippines flooding

High waves whipped up by hurricanes can reach land as long as a week before the storm strikes. In 1988, Manila in the Philippines was hit by a typhoon which caused severe flooding. Survivors were forced to cling to the inner tubes of tyres to avoid drowning (below).

A hurricane is fuelled by a flow of warm, moist air. Moving over a tropical ocean at speeds of 15-50 kph, it begins to die away only when it reaches land, where there is no supply of its fuel – water vapour. Yet it is just when it hits land that the hurricane is most destructive, bringing not only screaming winds but also huge waves.

SURGING

STORM SURGE

As the hurricane nears land, waves up to 10m high are whipped up by the storm to crash onto the shore. Beneath the hurricane's eye, a mound of water builds up. Millions of cubic metres of water are sucked upwards by low air pressure in the eye. This is called the storm surge. When it smashes ashore, low-lying land around the coast is flooded, towns are destroyed and animals and people are carried away.

Dune defences

ON CLOSER INSPECTION – *Ships under attack*

At sea, hurricane winds can create waves up to 25m high. Many ships have been lost in these stormy seas in the past (right). In 1944, the US Navy's Pacific fleet was crushed by Typhoon Cobra, which sank three destroyers and damaged many ships.

SEAS

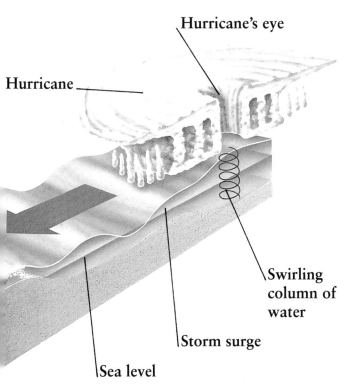

Hurricane's eye

Hurricane

Swirling column of water

Storm surge

Sea level

Since 1970 the Ganges region has been hit by other powerful cyclones. In 1991 250,000 people died in flooding caused by a hurricane even more powerful than that of 1970. About 10 million people were left homeless, without food or drinkable water.

A COUNTRY IS CREATED

The low-lying area around the mouth of the River Ganges in southern Asia is at great risk from cyclones from the Indian Ocean. In 1970, this region in Pakistan was destroyed by a cyclone (below). Over 500,000 people died when the storm surge struck. People felt their government had not helped enough after the disaster, so in 1971 they voted to be independent of Pakistan, and a new country, Bangladesh, was born.

A tornado or "twister" is a violently spinning column of air. Tornadoes are much smaller than hurricanes – but much more powerful. In the funnel of a tornado, winds spiral round at up to 450 kph. Tornadoes form on land and can travel at 100 kph, sucking up dust and leaving a trail of destruction.

Fast and furious

Fortunately tornadoes do not last long – usually about 15 minutes, though some can last for several hours. Despite this, the damage they do, as seen above in Lake Erie, USA in 1924, is still devastating.

TWISTER!

SPIRALS OF DESTRUCTION

Tornadoes are formed in thunderclouds by winds blowing into each other from opposite directions. The winds create a spinning funnel of air, inside which warm air rises at great speed. As the funnel tightens, the winds pick up speed. The spiral of air dips down from the bottom of the cloud towards the Earth. When it touches ground, it acts like a giant vacuum cleaner to suck up dust and debris. The tornado weaves across the land, destroying everything in its path.

A waterspout (right) is a funnel of air which stretches down from a cloud over the sea. Like tornadoes suck up soil and debris, waterspouts take up huge amounts of water.

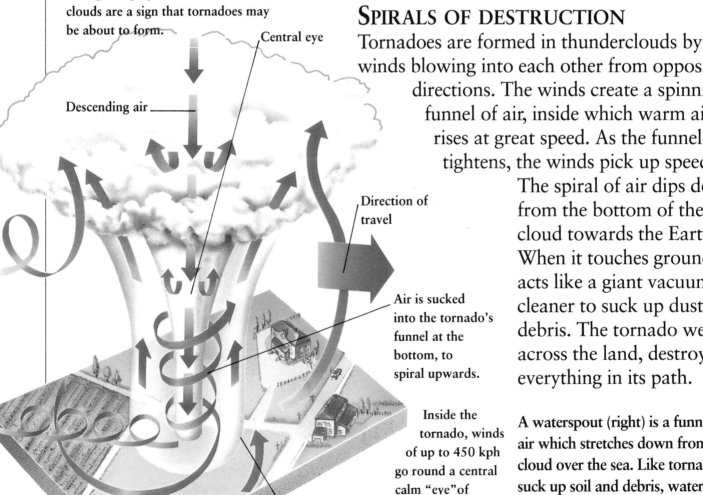

Strange bulging clouds called mamatus clouds are a sign that tornadoes may be about to form.

Central eye

Descending air

Direction of travel

Air is sucked into the tornado's funnel at the bottom, to spiral upwards.

Inside the tornado, winds of up to 450 kph go round a central calm "eye" of descending air.

Dust envelope

On Closer Inspection
– *The riddle of crop circles*

The origins of crop circles, flattened areas of corn, are mysterious. It has even been said that they are caused by aliens! Some people think that they are caused by weak whirlwinds – about 60 of these small tornadoes form a year in Britain.

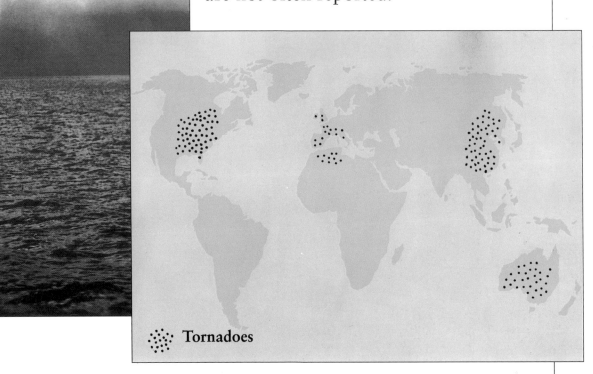

Tornadoes Around the World

As the map shows, tornadoes occur in many parts of the world, although they are rare in Africa and India. The most powerful tornadoes occur in the United States. European tornadoes are small and weak compared to those in America. They cause little damage and are not often reported.

∴∴∴ Tornadoes

In danger!

During warm, humid weather tornadoes occur almost every week in Tornado Alley. Little can be done to protect buildings or vehicles (below) in the path of a twister. The safest place is under the ground. Many houses in Tornado Alley have strong basement shelters.

Tornadoes produce the fastest winds on Earth, tearing roofs from buildings and lifting cars, trucks and even aeroplanes and hurling them through the air. The powerful winds around the eye of a tornado are so strong that buildings in the whirlwind's path can literally explode.

TRAIL OF

TORNADO ALLEY

"Tornado Alley" is in the southern United States stretching from Texas to Missouri where twisters often form. Up to 700 occur in these plains each year, sometimes in groups called "swarms". In 1965, a swarm of 37 tornadoes formed in nine hours in Tornado Alley, killing 271 people and causing huge damage. Even back in 1924, people were coping with the effects of living in Tornado Alley (see below).

ON CLOSER INSPECTION
– Desert devils

Dust devils are strong tornadoes that pass over desert areas. These swirling columns of air pick up sand or dust, and are usually about 30m high. The swirling sand makes the air seem cloudy.

DESTRUCTION

Is it possible?

There are many tales of freak damage caused by tornadoes. In Italy, in 1981, a tornado plucked a sleeping baby from its pram and carried it 100m through the air before putting it safely on the ground again. The child was still asleep! In 1931, in Minnesota, USA, a twister snatched up an express train and dropped it back to earth 25m away. Another carried a whole church steeple 10km!

A tornado in Java moves across the ocean.

A tornado lasts only minutes and leaves behind a thread of destruction. The damage caused by a hurricane, which may rage for hours and even days, is very much greater. A violent hurricane unleashes as much energy every second as the atom bomb that destroyed Hiroshima in Japan in 1945.

AFTER THE

The cost
Around the world each year many hurricanes strike land, causing billions of pounds of damage. Above we see south China in 1991 where many homes were destroyed by a typhoon.

A DEVASTATED LANDSCAPE
After a hurricane, roofs and buildings are scattered and vehicles tossed aside. Power and communication lines may be down and water supplies cut off. The first priority for emergency workers is to rescue survivors (left). Food and water must be brought in. In remote areas rescue parties may take days to arrive, and emergency supplies may have to be dropped by aeroplane.

CLEARING UP
Rescue workers must try to stop more lives being lost. Dangerous buildings must be made safe, power cables must be repaired and roads cleared. Water supplies must be restored. Then the clearing up begins. Damage such as this (right), caused by Hurricane David, can take months, even years to repair.

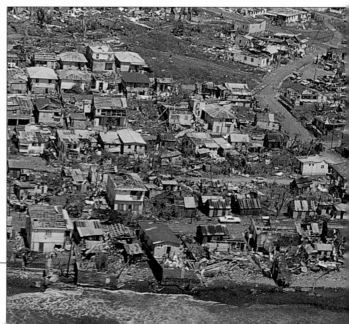

HURRICANE

Galveston, 1900 – a port in ruins

Low-lying coastal areas are often worst hit by hurricanes, due to flooding from storm surges (see pages 14-15). In 1900 the town of Galveston in Texas was a flourishing port. Yet the town's highest point was less than 3m above sea level. In September 1900 a huge hurricane hit Galveston (below). Floodwaters 6m deep hit the port. High winds destroyed Galveston, leaving 10,000 people homeless.

HURRICANE GILBERT DOES ITS WORST IN ST LUCIA

Hurricane Gilbert, the most powerful hurricane on record, struck the Caribbean islands in 1988. Vital crops were destroyed and flimsy shanty towns demolished (above), leaving thousands homeless.

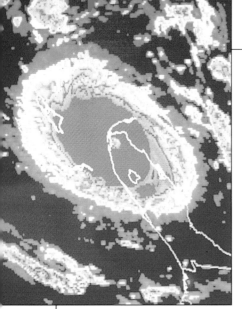

Today weather experts all around the world keep a close eye on storms which may develop into hurricanes. Even with modern methods, however, experts cannot predict the path of a hurricane with great accuracy. Prevailing winds may cause a hurricane to swerve from its predicted course, and strike anywhere within a range of 150km.

Eyes in space
Weather satellites send pictures of changing cloud patterns back to Earth. From space, hurricanes resemble vast whirling Catherine Wheels of cloud. This satellite image shows the development of Hurricane Andrew in August 1992 in Florida, USA.

TRACKING

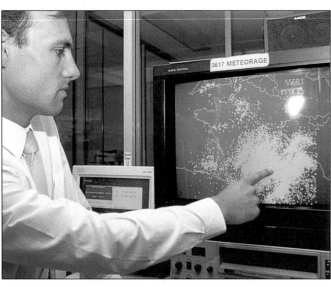

CLOUD WATCHING
Since Roman times, people have watched the clouds above Earth (below) to predict the weather. Recently, however, cloud-watching methods have become much more sophisticated. Today, scientists study photographs of cloud formations taken from satellites orbiting high above the Earth (right).

TECHNOLOGY OF TODAY
There are 10,000 permanent weather stations around the world, exchanging information about changing weather patterns. This information is fed into computers, and pictures such as this (above), of the 1987 storm in northern Europe, are produced.

ON CLOSER INSPECTION
– Hurricane detective

Grady Norton was chief hurricane forecaster for the US Weather Bureau from 1935-54, with an uncanny knack for predicting the path of hurricanes. He died in 1954 while tracking Hurricane Hazel, when high winds and high tides caused the river Potomac to rise 2.75m above normal (right).

HURRICANES

Flying high
Weather planes, like the one shown here, fly into hurricanes to measure wind speed, temperature and humidity (the level of moisture in the air). The instruments are mounted on a long probe so that they are not disturbed by turbulence from the plane's propellers. They can also take three-dimensional pictures of the atmosphere.

Weather buoys at sea, planes, balloons and rockets are also used to gather information and check on the development of hurricanes.

SATELLITE INFORMATION

Two kinds of satellites are used to observe Earth's weather from space. Polar satellites circle the Earth from Pole to Pole. Geostationary satellites keep pace with the Earth's rotation to maintain a fixed position above the Equator, from where they view a wide area of the planet's surface.

Nothing can divert a hurricane. However, meteorologists issue warnings, so that people in the path of a storm can leave or prepare themselves as much as possible. Strong sea defences and hurricane shelters also provide protection.

Sea defences

On coasts around the world, sea walls and dams have been built to reduce the risk of flooding caused by hurricanes (see pages 14-15). Heaps of concrete blocks piled against the sea wall also help to absorb wave energy in Japan, as we can see above.

STORM

BANGLADESH PREPARES

There are many cyclones in Bangladesh. People there are too poor to build houses with built-in hurricane shelters. However, since the cyclone disaster of 1970, communal hurricane shelters have been built on concrete stilts 4m high. People also prepare for flooding by using sandbags to prevent floodwaters from spreading.

The Thames Barrier was built to protect the city of London, England from floodwaters. It was completed in 1984.

ON CLOSER INSPECTION
– *Chasing the hurricane*

Hurricane chasers scan weather reports and guess where the storm will go, so they can go there to experience the full fury of nature. This dangerous activity is discouraged by the authorities!

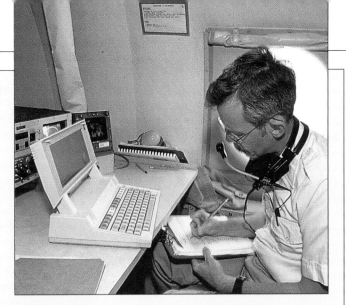

ALERT!

POOR MAN...

In developing countries such as Bangladesh or parts of Indonesia, less money is available for emergency services and rescue vehicles, such as boats and helicopters. Houses are often built of flimsy materials. The devastation caused by hurricanes is likely to be greater there. In Indonesia, houses may be built on stilts (left) to keep them out of the way of flood waters.

RICH MAN...

Rich countries like the United States are better prepared for hurricanes than some poorer countries. More money is spent in the USA on precautions against storm damage, and houses are sturdily built, with storm shutters (left) and basement shelters. In Florida, on the south-east coast, evacuation routes are always posted, so when warnings are issued, people can leave quickly.

Even with modern equipment at our disposal (see pages 22-3), some storms and hurricanes are difficult to predict. Some hurricanes increase in strength or change course unexpectedly. At other times, storm warnings are not taken seriously enough or are issued too late for people in the hurricane's path to take effective action.

UNPRED

Early warning?

In April 1991, a terrible cyclone hit Bangladesh, leaving ten million people homeless (above) and killed up to 250,000. Although warnings were given out, many people in this poor country had neither radios nor television, so they did not hear the warnings.

A CYCLONE FOR CHRISTMAS

On Christmas Eve 1974, a cyclone alert was issued for northern Australia.
A powerful cyclone named Tracey had developed off the northern coast. In the port of Darwin, people took little notice of the warning because of the coming holiday. Early on Christmas morning, the full force of Cyclone Tracey struck Darwin. The town was flattened – 90 per cent of buildings were destroyed (left), and Darwin had to be almost entirely rebuilt.

ON CLOSER INSPECTION
– *Hurricane parties*

In the 1950s and 60s on the south-eastern coast of the United States some people went to hurricane parties. Party-goers met to watch hurricanes rather than fleeing danger. In 1969, Hurricane Camille changed course to wreck an apartment where a party was held. Twenty-three people died.

I CTABLE

THE GREAT STORM OF 1987

Britain and mainland Europe do not experience true hurricanes. Yet the storm of 1987, is often called a hurricane because of its hurricane-force winds. British forecasters tracking the storm believed that the high winds would die down before reaching Britain, but in fact the opposite happened. By the time the gale hit Britain during the night of October 15-16, wind speed had built to 150 kph.

South-east England was worst affected. In all 19 people were killed. The main damage was to trees and buildings (above and right). Fifteen million trees were blown down. Normandy and Brittany in north-west France were also badly hit.

Polar problems

In the 1980s and 90s a rise in temperatures was reported worldwide. Some scientists predict that by 2050 world temperatures will rise by 4°C. This could melt the polar icecaps (below), increasing sea levels. This would mean serious flooding and put new areas at risk from storm surges caused by hurricanes.

Since the 1960s, scientists have noted that there has been an unusual number of violent storms and droughts across the world. This has led some scientists to think that the Earth is experiencing global warming – changing climates worldwide. This could mean more hurricanes since more regions would have a climate suitable for tropical storms.

STORMY

LIVING IN A GREENHOUSE

Global warming is caused by an increase in the "greenhouse effect"– gases in Earth's atmosphere act like the glass in a greenhouse, letting the Sun's rays in to heat the Earth but preventing all the heat from escaping back to space. The greenhouse effect occurs naturally and is essential to life on Earth. But man-made air pollution (left) is increasing the effect.

The main greenhouse gas is carbon dioxide, which occurs naturally but is also produced by vehicle exhausts and the burning of fossil fuels. As these gases increase in the atmosphere, more heat is trapped and temperatures rise.

Forty per cent of Bangladesh is less than 1m above sea level. If sea levels rise, scientists predict that by 2030 half the country could be underwater (right). Florida and New York in the US as well as Holland and London, England may also be at risk.

FUTURE

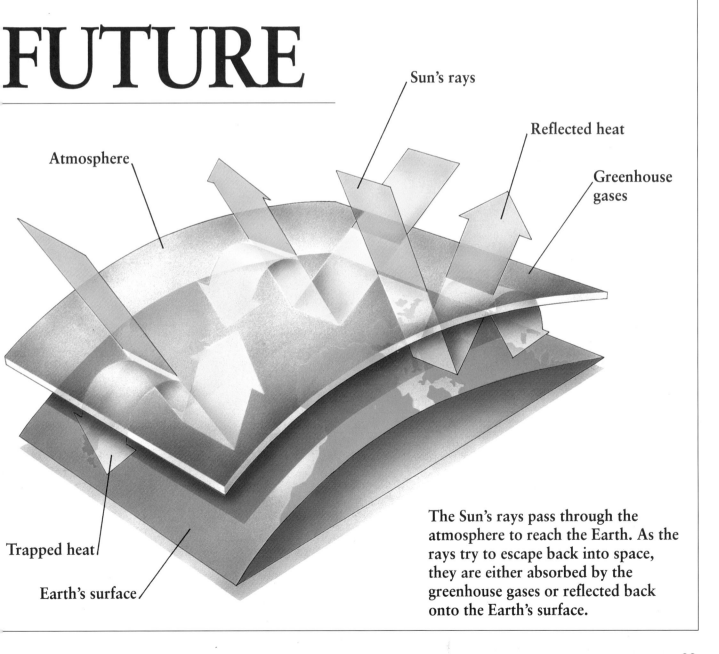

Atmosphere

Sun's rays

Reflected heat

Greenhouse gases

Trapped heat

Earth's surface

The Sun's rays pass through the atmosphere to reach the Earth. As the rays try to escape back into space, they are either absorbed by the greenhouse gases or reflected back onto the Earth's surface.

Long Island, USA after the 1938 cyclone.

CHRONOLOGY OF MAJOR HURRICANES AND TORNADOES

1737 A cyclone and storm surge struck Bengal in India, killing 300,000 people.

1900 A hurricane and storm surge devastated Galveston in Texas, USA killing about 6,000 people and leaving 10,000 homeless.

1938 A hurricane struck New England and Long Island, USA causing great destruction. About 600 people died.

1944 The US fleet in the Pacific was hit by Typhoon Cobra. Many ships were damaged.

1963 Hurricane Flora struck the Caribbean islands of Haiti, Cuba and the Dominican Republic, causing more than 7,000 deaths.

1965 The Palm Sunday Tornado Outbreak killed 271 people in Tornado Alley in the USA.

90 per cent of the town's buildings.

1974 Hurricane Fifi struck Honduras in Central America, bearing heavy rains. Eight thousand people died.

1979 Hurricane David struck Puerto Rico, America's south-east

London, England after the 1987 "hurricane".

Charleston, USA after Hurricane Hugo in 1989.

1969 Hurricane Camille struck seven states in the USA and killed more than 250 people.

1970 In one of the world's worst natural disasters, a cyclone and storm surge killed more than 500,000 people in Bangladesh.

1974 Cyclone Tracey struck Darwin in Australia, destroying

coast and the Dominican Republic, causing 4,000 deaths.

1988 Hurricane Gilbert, the most powerful on record, hit the West Indies and Mexico, killing about 300 people.

1991 A cyclone and storm in Bangladesh claimed 250,000 human lives.

GLOSSARY

Air pressure The weight of all the air in the atmosphere pressing down on the Earth.

Atmosphere The layer of gases that surrounds our planet and provides some of the conditions needed for life on Earth.

Beaufort scale Scale used to measure wind speed by describing the visible effects that winds produce.

Condense To change from a gas or vapour into a liquid, through cooling.

Coriolis effect The paths of the world's winds are deflected (bent) by the rotation of the Earth.

Cyclone The name for tropical storms when they occur in the Indian Ocean.

Depression An area of low air pressure.

Doldrums An area of low pressure along the Equator where the trade winds meet. Winds are calm and very light here.

Dust devil A swirling column of dust or sand caused by a desert whirlwind.

Evacuate To move people away from an area of danger such as a region threatened by a hurricane.

Evaporate To change from a liquid into a gas or vapour through being heated.

Eye Region of calm air in the centre of a hurricane, surrounded by spinning winds.

Global warming A rise in temperatures around the world, caused by the build-up of carbon dioxide and other "greenhouse gases" in the atmosphere.

Greenhouse effect The warming of the Earth's atmosphere caused by certain gases which trap heat from the Sun and prevent it escaping from the Earth back into space.

Humidity The amount of moisture (water vapour) in the air.

Hurricane A revolving tropical storm. Hurricanes are also known as typhoons and tropical cyclones.

Hurricane-force wind Wind speeds over 117kph, force 12 on the Beaufort scale.

Meteorologist Scientist who studies the weather.

Roaring forties Westerly winds which rage constantly in the southern hemisphere. They occur at latitude of 40°.

Storm surge Mound of water which builds up beneath the eye of a hurricane.

Tornado A funnel-shaped whirlwind of air extending down from a thundercloud. Also called a twister.

Trade winds Ships carrying goods around the world used these winds that blew to the Equator from the north or south-east.

Typhoon The name for hurricanes that form in the Pacific Ocean.

Waterspout A tornado that forms over water and sucks a column of water into the air.

Water vapour Water in the form of an invisible gas.

Wind A movement of air from one place to another.

INDEX

Photo credits